Retfor

GW00457733

on old picture pos

Angela and Greg Franks

1. E.L. Scrivens published this multi-view postcard of Retford, which was postally used in August 1921. All the pictures were available as individual cards.

Designed and Published by
Reflections of a Bygone Age
Keyworth, Nottingham
1993

Printed by
Adlard Print and Typesetting Services,
Ruddington, Notts.

Edgar Welchman came to Retford in 1905, taking premises in Exchange Street before opening the shop on Grove Street that still exists today, owned by Edgar's grandson John.

The mid-Edwardian period was the boom time for picture postcards, and Welchman soon began to realise their potential in Retford with a marvellous range of cards, the photographs for which he took himself on expeditions to surrounding areas as well as the town itself. Edgar's brother Howard worked alongside him for a while (hence the 'Welchman Bros.' on many of the postcards) before opening his own business in Gainsborough, an enterprise which ended in the early 1930s.

After the first world war, Edgar's son Leslie helped him with the photography and postcard publishing, but the card boom was over and Leslie's interest was more into radios. He began making these as a hobby, which rapidly became a business, and the shop changed character, particularly after 1945; in fact photographic work stopped entirely in the early 1960s, and the shop consolidated its radio/TV sales.

Edgar retired from the business in 1935; Leslie went into the fire service, and during the second world war his wife Vera looked after the shop. Their son John, the present owner, served his apprenticeship with Pye before coming back to Retford in 1961 and taking over all the servicing. His own son Spencer works in the shop now, the fourth generation of Welchmans there.

The postcard above shows the shop in its photographic days. The two side windows feature a fine display of cards, including some of the ones in this book. The little girl in the right centre window is Edgar's daughter Phyllis.

(thanks to John Welchman for the information and loan of the card).

ISBN 0 946245 68 1

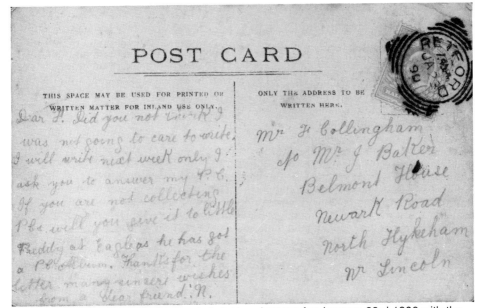

2. A clear strike of an old 'squared circle' hand stamp for January 23rd 1906 with the year figures '06' inverted. The message illustrates how popular postcards were: *"Dear F. ...... If you are not collecting PCs will you give it to little Freddy at Eagle as he has got a PC album".*

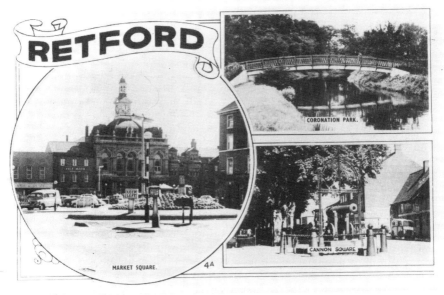

3. Retford Paper Co. published this multi-view, probably in the 1950s.

INTRODUCTION

The first twenty years of this century were a time of postcard mania. Not only were cards a cheap and efficient means of communication before the telephone was in common use but they were also enthusiastically collected. It is due to this intense interest that we are able to present Retford as it was in the not too distant past.

Grouped together the pictures show an attractive country town with a long and distinguished history revealed in its ancient churches, fine public buildings, spacious square and great occasions. But that is not all; for postcards have also survived of humbler folk and ordinary houses. Many of the cards were published locally by A. Hinkins, A. Hodson, Holoran & Co. and Chas. Taylor. However, one name stands out among all the others; that of Edgar Welchman, later Welchman Brothers, without whose photographs this book would hardly be possible.

In 1909, Leonard (see illus. 49) wrote: "This is a very swell place" and indeed through the medium of the postcards we can see Retford at a time when the Great North Road ran through the town, aristocrats still lived in the Dukeries and Retford's markets and shops were a major centre for the outlying villages. Successful industrialists from towns such as Sheffield built fine houses in Retford and the prosperous local inns were full of visitors.

It is hoped that this book will revive many happy memories for older inhabitants. Others will find it very rewarding to go round the town using the book as a guide and reference. Many places have disappeared without a trace; others are recorded in name only but there is much that remains in spite of the great increase in population – less than four thousand in 1901 and over twenty thousand at the present time. People will recognise their own homes or the place where they were born or spent their childhood.

It is the pictures which tell the story; the captions are there as a guide and a reminder. Above all it is intended that the book will complement others published about Retford and contribute to the rediscovery of the town and resurgence of interest in its past.

Angela and Greg Franks
March 1993

Acknowledgements: We would like to thank Mrs Carol Dunk at the Retford Tourist Information Centre, Mr. Malcolm Dolby M.A., Curator of the Bassetlaw Museum, members of staff at the Railway Station and lunchtime regulars at the "Northern Inn", all of whom were most helpful.

Most of the postcards in this book come from the Tim Farr collection, and we are extremely grateful for their loan.

Back cover (top): Market Day at Retford on a postcard by Ashley, sent to Southport in August 1906.

(bottom): Church Gate in the 1950s, with the "Vine" Inn, selling Worksop Ales, on the left. 'Arjay' series card no. 414.

4. C.W. Faulkner's heraldic card shows the elegant falcons combatant which were originally on East Retford's crest. However, as a result of a private joke, the falcons became humble choughs when the coat-of-arms was granted in 1940. The town motto is a fitting one; *"Vetustas Dignitatum Generat"*. (Antiquity generates dignity).

5. Since this view was taken about 1910, Ollerton Road has changed greatly. A few houses, similar to those in the picture, survive close to where Ollerton and West Carr Roads merge. The immediate surroundings are now industrialised. Card by Edgar Welchman and numbered 128.

6. Station Road looks very much the same today as it did in this 1920s postcard. The wall on the left hand side borders the railway sidings. Doncaster Rotophoto Co. postcard no. 200-26.

S 5123 · RETFORD STATION.

7. Looking north on Retford Station in 1913. The main platform on the right has altered very little but the one on the left no longer exists. The whole junction was re-organised and three new platforms added in 1964. W.H. Smith 'Kingsway' series card. Smith's published postcards of all the railway stations where they had bookstalls.

8. The Prince of Wales at Retford Station during his visit in 1923. Nowadays royal visitors arrive at R.A.F. Finningley and approach the town in a motorcade. Published by A. Hinkins, Retford.

Victoria Road, Retford.

9. Built in 1896 by the Trinity Hospital Trustees to provide easier access to the station, Victoria Road retains many of its old houses and the gap left for odd numbers 1-11 still exists. The tall chimney of the Albert Paper Mill on Albert Road has been demolished. Valentine of Dundee published the card, which was used in 1917.

10. This Welchman Bros. view of Albert Road was taken from the corner of Cobwell Road opposite the "Northern" Inn. The vehicle, which is outside the inn, is probably a fast two-wheeled chaise, the equivalent of a modern sports car.

11. Another road built in Victorian times to create a better route to the station. Queen's Street is instantly recognisable in this Doncaster Rotophoto card no. 200-42.

Queen's Street, Retford.

12. A different angle on Queen's Street clearly shows the poor state of the roads which were not yet metalled. Published about 1908 by H. Hodson of Market Place, Retford.

GIRLS' HIGH SCHOOL, RETFORD.

13. The Girls' High School as it appeared in the 1920s. The present school was established by the County Council in 1913 but in 1979 it amalgamated with Hallcroft Girls' School and is now The Elizabethan High School.

S 8153   THE LOCK WOODCOCK'S BRIDGE.   RETFORD.

14. A charming picture of West Retford lock on the Chesterfield Canal. Thomas Woodcock, after whom the bridge was named, owned a coalyard and the "Boat" Inn nearby. The row of cottages on the left is the quaintly-named Protestant Place. The card was posted on 7th November, 1914, and published by W.H. Smith.

A. Hinkins, Photo.　　　　　TRINITY HOSPITAL, RETFORD.

15. Trinity Hospital has a long and distinguished history. Originally the site of West Retford Hall, the Hospital was rebuilt in 1828, with further additions in 1872. Until the 1970s, elderly inmates of the Hospital, known as "brethren", could be identified by their distinctive cloaks. The building was designed by Edward Blore, better known for his work on the Lambeth and Buckingham Palaces. Card published by A. Hinkins of Retford.

Babworth Road, Retford

16. The opening of the Babworth Road Bridge in 1936 created a quiet cul-de-sac where once had been a very busy level crossing. The streetscape in this Valentine's card, postmarked 29th September 1922, has scarcely changed.

17. A rather bleak view of Lime Tree Avenue published by Welchman (No.97) and posted in 1907. The original saplings are now mature trees and the Avenue, which has been completed by the addition of modern bungalows, is a pleasant leafy road.

18. Another Welchman card no.178, showing the spacious Baptist Church built in 1872 and indicating the strength of the Baptist movement in Retford which goes back to the seventeenth century.

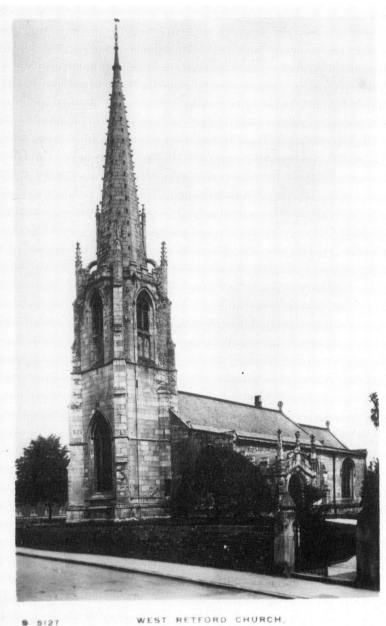

S 5127   WEST RETFORD CHURCH.

19. The lovely fourteenth century spire of Saint Michael's Church, West Retford, was described by the great Victorian architect Pugin, who helped restore the church, as a poem in stone. This view, taken from Rectory Road, was postally used on 18th October 1911 and published by W.H. Smith.

Valentine's Series   Bridgegate, Retford

20. This view of Bridgegate shows the "Newcastle Arms", one of the many coaching inns on the busy Great North Road. Carriers' carts, one of which is parked outside the inn, were a common sight in Edwardian Retford as they plied their trade between the town and the outlying villages. The elaborate Victorian building on the left is now a hairdressers. Valentines card, postally used in 1905.

BRIDGE GATE, RETFORD

21. Taken from the corner outside the "White Hart" and looking north, this card was posted in 1957. Many buildings along Bridgegate bear the intertwined initials 'T.H.' referring to improvements carried out in the area by the Trinity Hospital Trustees with money gained from land they developed after the coming of the railway. Another Valentine-published card.

RIVER IDLE, WEST RETFORD

22. A very pleasant view of hopeful young anglers fishing at the bridge over the River Idle, West Retford. Published by W.H. Smith, in their 'Kingsway' series.

CANNON SQUARE, RETFORD

23. Captured at the siege of Sebastopol in 1858, the cannon was installed in Retford in 1859. It was dismantled along with railings during World War 2 but escaped being melted down and was restored to its traditional place in 1949. Jackson & Sons, Grimsby, published this photographic card.

24. Posted at South Leverton on 5th December 1906, this view of Chapelgate gives a clear picture of the "Crown" Inn. The inn, dating from the mid-seventeenth century, was once Retford's most important coaching inn and had a colourful and varied past. It is now the offices of a building society. Welchman card no. 172.

25. St. Swithun's, the Corporation Church, a well-known landmark in the centre of Retford, has been frequently added to and restored since the original was built in the middle ages. The railings were removed in 1942 as part of the war effort. Doncaster Rotophoto Co. no. 200-71, posted in September 1924.

26. A dismal view of Cannon Square and the church. The roads around the square in 1918, when this card was posted, were in a very poor state, being dusty in summer and muddy in winter although the busy crossings were swept regularly. Published by Jackson & Son, Grimsby.

27. Looking from Cannon Square across the Market Place in the 1930s. The Yorkshire Penny Bank on the right is now the Yorkshire Bank and the A1 is signposted in both directions. Cash and Co., which is on the left in the background, was part of a national chain of shoe shops.

28. Retford's spacious Market Place with its Victorian a
Postmarked Retford, 19th August 1908, this postcard sh
the right are standing outside what is now the Lloyds Ba
of today's Abbey National offices whilst the stall with the
sway' series no. 2402.

gian facades comes as a pleasant surprise to visitors.
square at the height of the Edwardian era. The boys on
corner of Grove Street. The tea adverts are on the wall
iped awning is an ice-cream vendor. W.H. Smith 'King-

Market Day, Retford.

Holoran & Co., Retford.

29. A very early view of the Market in Retford published by the local firm of Holoran & Co. and posted in January 1905. This card shows clearly the variety of horse-drawn vehicles used by traders whilst at the left can be seen a range of agricultural implements – a reminder of Retford's rural past.

Market Place, Retford.

30. Cars could park in the Market Place until 1977 when it became a pedestrianised area. Among the shops on the right are Dunn's (boot and shoe shop). Melia's (food distributors), and that very famous local firm, Clarks of Retford. A Valentine card, postally used in May 1938.

200.39. White Hart. Retford.

31. The "White Hart" has stood on the corner of Market Place and Bridgegate since the early eighteenth century. It has adapted well to many changing situations and became very prosperous when the Great North Road passed its doors. The outbuildings and stabling at the back must have been busy when eighteen coaches a day departed for destinations such as Boston and London. Doncaster Rotophoto Co. postcard no. 200-39.

32. Perfectly captured on an Edgar Welchman card (no.27), George V inspects a guard of the Sherwood Rangers while Queen Mary watches from the platform outside the Town Hall on June 26th, 1914. Just a matter of weeks later Britain was plunged into the Great War.

33. On the same day a large crowd, some of them standing on a handcart to get a better view, gathered to see the King and Queen. Marshal & Son, to the left of the Town Hall, later became Woolworths. Published by Welchman, card no.19.

34. Another patriotic crowd awaiting the arrival of the Prince of Wales *(see illus. 8)* in 1923. They are obviously not deterred by rather damp conditions clearly shown in this Edgar Welchman card.

35. This time everyone is celebrating George V's Silver Jubilee on 6th May 1935. The row of shops in the background were (from the right) Baines & Son (sports outfitters), the "White Hart" Hotel, Smith, Foster & Co. (grocers, wine and spirit merchants) and the York County Savings Bank. A further example of Welchman's work.

TOWN HALL, RETFORD.

36. Built in 1868, the Town Hall was the headquarters of the Corporation and Borough of Retford until local government reorganisation in 1974 when Retford became part of Bassetlaw District Council. To the right is The Old Bank, once Foljambe's Bank, which was purchased by the Town Council as offices in 1926 when the ornate redbrick frontage was added. Rotophoto Co. card, postally used in March 1910.

37. The War Memorial which was erected in 1921 to commemorate those who lost their lives in the Great War 1914-1918. Card published by Scrivens of Doncaster.

38. John Wesley visited Retford in 1779 and the growth of the Methodist movement in the town is reflected in the splendid Wesleyan Chapel on Grove Street, built in 1879. It replaced an earlier one on the same site and can seat 1,000 people. Scrivens postcard of 1920s vintage, but not used until 1942.

39. Grove Street. On the right hand corner is the Great Central Railway Booking Office and the Talbot Vaults, Home Brewery – now a bank. On the left, a good variety of shops; H. Dudley (glass & china), Hinde's (cycle agents) and in the centre is Welchman Brothers (photographers), the publishers of this card which was posted 2nd October 1909. (No. 298). Welchman's shop now sells electrical goods.

40. A busy view of Grove Street in the thirties showing a further range of shops including a traditional hardware store. Further along on the left is Clark's (dyers and dry cleaners) the nationally famous firm which was established in Retford in 1798. Published by Scrivens, G6-40.

41. Saint Swithun's Church of England Aided Primary School was built in 1858 and was originally the National School. Welchman Bros. card, no.267.

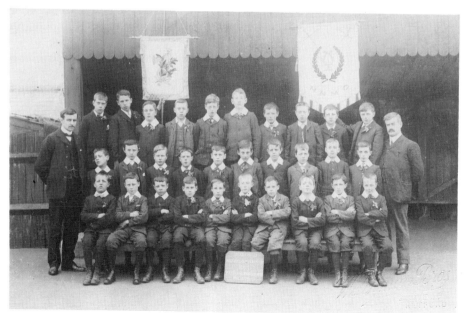

42. Winning the North Notts. Music Competition in 1907 was a solemn affair if the group in this picture of boys from the National School are anything to judge by. Once again Welchman Bros. recorded an important moment in the lives of local inhabitants.

CAROLGATE, RETFORD

43. *"Temptation"* is showing at the Picture House Theatre on Carolgate and the children outside the toyshop have been distracted by the photographer who may well have owned the motorcycle sidecar combination. (It was a favourite vehicle with travelling photographers).

44. A later view of Carolgate taken in the 1950s. The "Pheasant" Hotel was demolished in 1973 to make way for Tesco's. Even though this is a fairly recent card, a great many changes have taken place in this corner of Retford in the intervening years. Arjay of Doncaster were the publishers of the card.

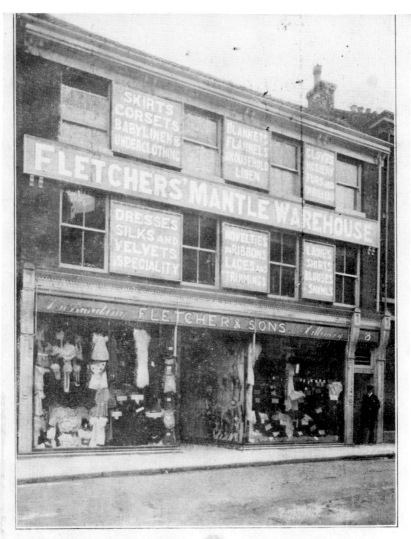

FLETCHER & SONS, Ltd.,

Drapers and House Furnishers,

RETFORD.

TELEPHONE NO. 24.

45. Fletcher's themselves published this card which was posted in 1907. This busy, well-known shop stood for many years on Carolgate where the firm had several separate premises. Robert Fletcher once owned Arlington House (now the site of New Street Car Park), which is remembered in the name Arlington Way.

46. An Edwardian view of London Road, although if it were not for the school railings it would be difficult to identify because this stretch of the road has changed so much. The two young ladies would be foolhardy to stroll along the middle of the road today! Published by E.L. Scrivens, no.6-12.

47. An unusual picture of the rear of the Grammar school taken by Welchman and posted in 1906. In that year there were 141 boys on roll which increased to 200 by the outbreak of war in 1914. Extensions and additions have altered this view drastically. The school is now a comprehensive with 750 pupils. (Welchman no.44)

48. The original grammar school was built on Chapelgate in the sixteenth century and the imposing Victorian building pictured here was erected on London Road in 1853. (Welchman no. 86, postally used 30th October, 1906).

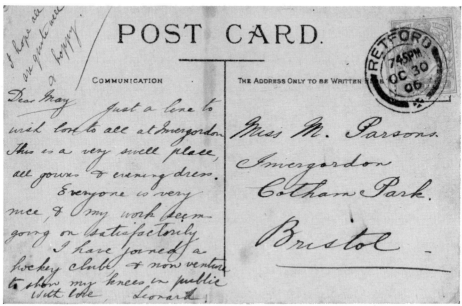

49. (reverse of the above). The message reads, *"Dear May, Just a line to wish love to all at Invergordon. This is a very swell place, all gowns and evening dress. Everyone is very nice and my work seems going on satisfactorily. I have joined a hockey club and now venture to show my knees in public, with love, Leonard."*

50. Storcroft House, London Road. Now a business school but originally built as a private house for a wealthy businessman. Welchman Bros. no.242 posted on 24th December 1906.

51. London Road where it crosses the railway, looking south. A 1920s view that has changed little apart from the volume of traffic. Published by Scrivens of Doncaster, no.V6-12.

52. Looking north along London Road. Edgar Welchman published this early view of the old "Nags Head" which has long since ceased to be a pub (it's now private housing), although the row of houses opposite remain. The card was posted in 1906.

53. All that survives of this corner of Edwardian Retford is the name, Winney Moor Park, a modern development of private housing. The lad in the foreground is standing alongside a hitching post which was an important piece of street furniture in the days of horse-drawn transport. This is the old London Road (A1) facing south; Bracken Lane is to the left and Winney (now Whinney) Moor Lane to the right. Card published by Welchman (no.48) and posted in 1906.

54. Another Welchman Brothers postcard (no.165), this time showing Saint Saviour's Anglican Church, built in 1829 to serve Retford's growing population. Welham Road on which the church stands is now very busy and the area is greatly changed.

55. Newcomers to Retford may have difficulty in recognising this view. It is necessary to go some way down Bolham Lane, past the new developments, in order to find these cottages which remain largely unaltered. Published by Welchman Brothers (no.280).

56. Pausing politely for the camera, the children of Richard Street stand quite casually in the middle of the road. There is not a motor vehicle in sight for when this picture was taken about 1909 there were only five cars registered in the town. Welchman card no. 55.

57. "Raspberry Terrace, Strawberry Road, New Town, 1885" reads the inscription on the plaque above the second front door. This Welchman postcard, no.93, posted in June 1909, does not do justice to a very pretty corner of Retford which still enjoys delightful views across open countryside. The card is captioned *"Strawberry Terrace"*, which was actually at the other end of Strawberry Road and is no longer there.

58. Posted in 1924, this view of Northfield Way was taken within a few years of the road being built. The road is unchanged apart from the welcome addition of mature trees. Published by Scrivens of Doncaster.

59. A view of Hallcroft Road (though titled West Furlong on the postcard) in 1928. The flat-roofed building to the right, once a branch of Clark's, disappeared along with the Post Office when the site was developed for housing.This card was published by Lilywhite of Halifax. *"This is a bit of Retford where I have been this week. I go home tomorrow,"* wrote the sender.